TABU

FREE YOUR MIND

Identifiers : ISBN 979-8-218-46185-0 (paperback)
Prolific Publications | Independently Published

Please Contact Author for any inquiries at **tabu.thebook@gmail.com**
www.tigressunleashed.com

Photographs, Illustrations, and Cover Design by Jessica M Webber
Author Images by Tyler McAuley

_THE
_ART
OF
_BEING
_UNLEASHED

PROLIFIC

SPECIAL DEDICATION

To my Underdogs & Loners

To be a lover, you have to be a fighter.
For if you don't fight for Love .. what are you actually fighting for?

The story of the lone wolf tends to be (fragmented) and glorified.
Think about it ... Who would consciously choose to walk amongst a dark forest alone? Only the wolf who has been exiled. Only the wolf who is strong enough to walk away from a pack that doesn't love and hunt like they do.

For only the lone wolf has a deep understanding of what it means to be the strongest lover and fighter - at the same time.

Keep making your way through that forest.
The truth shall rise and your real pack shall gather.
Because if your fight is strong, and the love is stronger ...
You can survive anything.

PRELUDE

Life, Love, Luxury, Light - These are our birthrights.
Tomorrow is guaranteed, yet never promised. So we must act now.
This next era is for the Brave Souls. The Chosen Ones.
The Ones who have been hidden in plain sight for quite some time.
Well ... now it's time. It's time to let your Light shine.
May this be a gentle reminder that : You got this ... We got this.

TABU TABLE OF CONTENTS

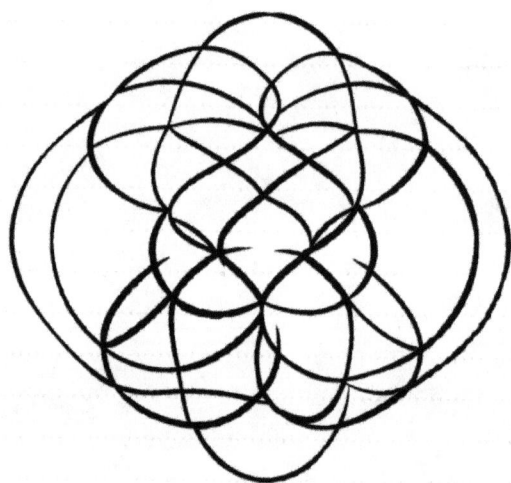

WELCOME

What is *The Art of Being Unleashed*? It's *TABU*. It's speaking my truth. My name is Prolific AKA the Tigress Unleashed. I was born with a wild spirit that can't be tamed. I follow my intuition and run towards any risk or challenge that calls my name. All of my experimentation and experience thus far has brought me to a point of enlightenment. I've realized that no matter how life is lived, there will always be challenges. And during times of immense challenge or resistance, one is often directed down a somber road. Truthfully, there is much to be learned among the dark alleys on somber road, yet it is wise to not stay for long.

Have you been in the shadows for too long? If so, get ready to learn how to turn darkness into light : Pain into Prosperity and Peace. Are you ready to learn how to accept and integrate both Light and Dark? If so, Welcome.

You have reached your Transcendence and Ascension.

Emerge yourself in this text with an open mind and open heart. My wish is to not influence you by who I am or what got me here, yet to inspire you with what I say. Every word comes straight from the heart. I am here to set others free. I believe it is time for us to experience a brighter world - a world full of more Freedom, Joy, and Love.

WELCOME

Take a deep breath.
Breathe in ... Breathe out ...
Let me show you how to ignite a flame within your soul : How to unleash.

TABU is designed to be read from beginning to end. However, not all will be called to do so. That means you have a specific message in here waiting for you. You'll find it.

My intention is that *The Art of Being Unleashed* inspires you to empower yourself and create a limitless frequency within your mind, body, and soul. I am here to remind you of your eternal and infinite power.

Welcome to my Reality.
This text is meant to inspire, not astray. To provide comfort, not conflict. Take what resonates and leave the rest behind.

STEP BY STEP

1
Life is Your Birthright

One must hold with unwavering confidence that life is your God-given birth-right.

"God". Bold stance for the first sentence. Yes, I know. I do believe there is a non-physical source at play that is the Creator of our existence. No matter your stance on this topic, I invite you to open your mind. I invite you to explore the idea that we are all being protected by a Higher Power with no specific definition. I invite you to open your mind to the idea that we are all meant to be here. May I ask ... Do you believe we are ALL protected and loved? Do you believe that it all works out in the end? ... Because I am here to tell you that we are - and it does.

One must deeply believe that you belong here. You have an innate right given to you at birth : the right to fully embody your true essence at any moment. The right to fully be alive! To be alive is to feel the world through all of your senses. To experience the beautifully mystic nature of Life; our connection. Our connection is key to our belonging. If you ever feel isolated, come back to your senses. Senses are God's gift to us. To touch, smell, see, taste, and feel is an underrated blessing. Through our senses not only do we find connection, but we also find creation. We get to create the life of our dreams by aligning with the sensations we desire to experience.

Due to the current programming of society, many of us have lost the ability to see that life is a phenomenon. We have been programmed to feel separated, isolated, wronged, fearful, and envious. These feelings have the power to entrap the human mind into thinking life is bad and that it will never be good. It also has the power to make some of us not want to be alive. Let me tell you : YOU ARE ALIVE AND YOU DESERVE GOOD THINGS.

We judge and compare naturally. We are constantly absorbing information and making choices, it's a natural part of life. However, comparison to the point of hating your own life or changing who you are just to "fit in" is an evil trap. Once we have fallen into the trap of comparison leading to resentment of self or others, it can be hard to escape. Once we change the core essence of who we are to become more digestible for others, we begin to disrespect our birthright and naturally disconnect ourselves from Source. Source can be seen as another word for God, or connection to self and the Universe.

Let's ground it back down. Do you agree we have been programmed to judge our lives based on external influence? We judge who has the best job, the biggest house, the newest car, the freshest clothes, the dream relationship, the perfect look, etc. Have you ever taken a moment to wonder why? Why are we all in competition with one another? When was the last time you had a pure thought about someone who seems more successful than you? Or do you view them with envy and jealousy? Do you let someone else's external projection of their life cause you to be dissatisfied with yours? These are important questions to ask yourself.

Now, I invite you to think about the phrase 'we are all one in the same.'

How does this make you feel? What are your immediate reactions to this statement? It's obvious we are not exactly the same, but all of us are human beings. That counts for something, right? By removing all external viewings and projections, at our core, we are all human. For me that indicates that not a single person in this world is more worthy or deserving than you are. Not a single person is better than you are. Although some of our lives are not the prettiest roadmap, it's a roadmap nonetheless. Keep your blinders on. Master your own map. It's a level playing field in the sense that we are all capable of achieving and breathing. So let's start there.

Life Is Your Birthright. It's a blessing to be alive. It's a blessing to have infinite opportunities that you get to create. It's a blessing to have the option to step into your fullest expression at any moment. It's time to understand that you alone is an entire army. Act like it. Strap your boots up and start marching to the beat of your own drum. Life is deserved. Life is precious. Life is meant to be lived. Nothing should stop you from living your life, and nothing can stop you ... as long as you don't let it.

If you're feeling overwhelmed or unworthy, focus on yourself.
Look in the mirror and remind yourself, "Life is my birthright."

2
There is No Good or Bad.
There Just Is.

In a world where we get praised and shamed, it's easy to fall into thinking life must be lived a certain way to be "good."

The truth is, there is no good. The truth is, Light and Dark are the same thing. The duality of life is just a reflection. Duality is Unity. Unity is Wholeness. It's the law of Oneness. We are all connected in this existence. We all experience the "good" and "bad," the Light and Dark. So why favor one over the other?

Life is meant to be experienced, not judged. We are curious, free-spirited beings at our core. We are meant to explore and try new things. We are meant to take risks, AKA leaps. At times these leaps will lead us off the edge of a cliff. And what's guaranteed if you fall off a cliff? It's going to hurt. We tend to be highly influenced and impacted after a risky leap leads to a harsh landing. Because what about being protected and loved, right? So why have I been punished with pain?

It's inevitable to make choices that create pain. It's a necessary part of our discovery process. We cannot evolve without lessons. We must learn what feels good for us; what works. We must also learn what feels bad to us; what doesn't work. These experiences create our life ... in its entirety.

We cannot get stuck in what happened instead of why it happened. "Everything happens for a reason," they say. Well actually, it does. Every experience is meant to teach you, reflect to you, or guide you. This is not to discredit any trauma you've lived through, or still may be living through. This is meant to shed a new light on your perspective of the situation. What you've felt is real. What you've seen cannot be unseen. What you've heard cannot be unheard. Unfortunately, you cannot erase it - it's not going anywhere. Fortunately, you have options on how you're going to deal with it. You have the choice to put down some of the weight you're carrying by shifting your thoughts about it. It all starts with the mind. It all starts within.

You must know that any mistake you've made isn't bad, nor does it make you bad. Again, mistakes are inevitable. We aren't perfect. Please know that it does not matter how big or small the mistake may seem ... You are not a bad person. You are human. Shit happens. Some of us received conditioned programming that set us up for failure and lots of harsh landings. Forgive yourself. Forgive others. Dust it off and keep moving. Begin to create your own programming. Do it for you - for your peace of mind, for your quality of life.

*Disclaimer : Forgiveness does not equal access. If someone in your life has truly treated you "bad", forgive them from a distance. Do not allow the "bad" moments to repeat in the name of not judging the human experience. Some things do need to be judged for your own well-being and safety.

"Good" vs "Bad" goes much deeper than painful experiences.

Let's talk taboo. Enjoying taboo things doesn't make you "bad" either! If you truly enjoy something that is considered not socially acceptable, oh well. Society has created a mold of what is "normal" and "good". Another scam. Break the mold. When you free yourself from trying to fit into a mold created by someone else, you free yourself. These molds are detrimental to our true nature. We must be allowed to explore and try new things without fear of judgment or punishment.

Remember it's your right to live your life to the fullest. However you wish to. Who cares what other people think. Let them judge you while you live your best life. Understand : It Just Is. It's all supposed to be here. It's Life. Our crazy, beautiful lives.

If you're feeling judged or shamed, come back to acceptance. You must tell yourself, "There is no good or bad, there just is."

3
Really ... It's Not That Serious.

Have you taken the time to realize it's not that deep?

Have you taken a swim in the emotion ocean recently? Scared? Uncertain? Heartbroken? Angry? Now you feel like you're drowning? Well, sometimes these emotions stay longer than necessary and trick you into thinking you're something you're not. These emotions may become too heavy to carry and sink you into depths of the ocean that seem inescapable. Emotions are strong and complex. The most powerful thing in the world is human emotion ... yet we are taught to run from them. Why do you think that is? Why run away from something so powerful?

When we feel our emotions, we no longer let them control us. By not allowing yourself to feel, you automatically block your intuitive and creative abilities. You suppress your true nature. You may convince yourself that what you're feeling isn't real, or that you don't have the time for it. Truthfully, it is real and you must make the time for it. Feeling and expressing your emotions will create space in your life to think about the things that actually matter to you.

When we hide from ourselves, we quickly develop patterns that make us feel safe. We tend to create a form of shelter and safety away from the strength of our emotions. We do this because the truth is not always easy to admit. There is a part of us obsessed with how things are perceived, and this side of us can easily be wounded. For instance : A child starts sobbing in the middle of school. All the other children start laughing at them. This child feels embarrassed because of their sadness. Instinctively a new pattern develops in order to feel safe. So now the child begins physically fighting others to validate and protect themselves. Hidden emotions and no one to turn to can cause improperly placed feelings. Sadness disguised as anger and aggression. Now the emotion has lost its truest expression and turned itself into a weapon. An example to think about... but not too deeply, it's just an example. An example of how one unpleasant experience can turn into a weight too heavy to carry.

Really ... It's Not That Serious. The key here is to remember by feeling our emotions and letting them go, we get to escape the mental prison of our own mind. We get to break through the barriers of stagnation and strife within oneself by remembering it's not that serious. Whenever you feel yourself drowning in the emotion ocean, remember to swim. Swim until you feel the pressure lifting off your chest. Life is meant to be felt. Feel it then let it go. Just keep swimming and swimming until you find your pocket of sunshine.

You are not alone. The emotion ocean has the capacity to hold us all. The emotions you are navigating, no matter how extreme, have been felt by another. Come back to your sense of belonging, your connection. Chances are whatever you are feeling right now, someone else has experienced it too. At times, returning to this knowing can lighten the load naturally.

Sounds great, but how? Are you currently in a place where feeling your emotions is uncomfortable, or you don't know how to? That's okay. Just know, one way or another, to feel it is to heal it. May I suggest writing? Pick up a pen, pencil, or keyboard. Sit down, take a deep breath, and begin to write down anything that comes to mind. It's personal, it's safe, and it's a great place to start being honest with yourself. Writing is a way to directly face your innermost being and get to know it. We are on a forever journey of discovery. Don't think about it too much. Just start. Anything great isn't built in a day.

If you're feeling somber and disassociated, come back to laughter.
Look in the mirror with a smile and say, "Really ... it's not that serious."

4
We Are Forever Young.

Yes, I know you've heard this before.

Truly think about the term "forever young." What does that mean to you? To me it means our bodies may age, but our heart stays the same. Our soul yearns to be listened to at every stage and every age. Now, what do I mean by this? I mean GO FOR IT. If you wake up one day and want to move across the country... do it. If you have a sudden urge to change career paths ... do it. If you have been with someone for years and decide the relationship is no longer right for you ... leave. If you need to confess your love for someone ... stop reading this right now and do it. Cliche to say, but life is short. Every day we wake up is a miracle because nothing in this life is promised.

The moral of the story is : let absolutely nothing stand in your way. Never let anyone tell you (not even yourself) that it is "too late" or you are "too old." At 5 years old and 85, we are still HERE. We are psychically alive. Just because we've made some orbits around the sun does not mean that we should stop living our life to the fullest. Take a moment to think about childhood. Remember how exciting experiencing new things was as a child? Your first ice cream cone, your first kiss. Remember those butterflies? That is innocence at its purest, most present form. We can forever keep that excitement in our hearts by living forever young. Forever ourselves. Forever listening to our own desires and honoring them.

We have free will. We have the freedom to make our own decisions at any moment. You know the feeling when you've made a decision and no longer feel the same about it? It's okay to change your mind at any time. If you believe "there's no going back" once you've made a decision or commitment to something - you are placing a limitation on what you can become. Use your inner wisdom as a compass to where you want to go. Stand tall, stand strong, stand forever young.

If you're feeling like it's "too late", come back to presence.
Go outside and declare to the world, "I am forever young."

5
Release the Grip.

I heard you want to free your mind...

Letting go of our personal attachments and comforts is not easy because it makes us feel vulnerable. So now the question is: how bad do you want it? The fear of being vulnerable is what keeps many trapped. The comfort of our patterns and possessions can hold us hostage. The key is to release. Release it all. Nothing ever stays the same anyways. Life is constantly moving and evolving all around us. The quicker we can accept the ever-evolving nature of life, freedom is on the other side.

For instance, imagine releasing time. This means you let go of knowing that time exists. Schedules, appointments, dates - throw it all away. It is crucial we discover how to take a moment to "be" instead of "do". We are not meant to always be on the clock. Sometimes the best thing you can do is let go. Release the attachment and rest. Set an alarm if you have to. You can schedule a moment in time to forget about time. Practice.

The same goes for personal relationships. If your best friend stops talking to you tomorrow, how would you feel? If your lover doesn't live up to your expectations, how do you react? Yes, these things will hurt. Pain and grief are more than likely when you lose someone, or when your needs get left unfulfilled. The goal is to learn to let it be. Feel the pain, feel the hurt, release the grip of your attachment and expectation, then move on with your life. I'm not telling you to "not care." No. You have the right to fight for what you believe in; what you love. I just ask that you keep in mind we all have free will. Which means we are not designed to control another human being. Save yourself the suffering and keep it flowing.

If you lost every material possession you owned right now, how would you feel? If you deleted all social media from your phone, how would you feel? If you had to spend a week alone in solitude, how would you feel? Do you see the grip? Do you see the intense attachment to external people and situations that is embedded within our programming? We have all agreed on the one truth of life : Nothing Stays the Same. So why is change, loss, and gain difficult to handle? Because we are too attached to how we expect it to look and feel. We create stories and excuses that validate our hidden desire to stay the same in this life. Constant motion can get exhausting. At times we crave a break. At times we may let our energy lay dormant in what we created in order to find stability. It's completely normal to find safety and security within material matters and within other people. Of course you are allowed to celebrate this. Just remember, your external world is simply a reflection of your inner world. Which means true safety and security must first be created from within.

What are you holding on to that's holding you back?
This is your invitation to physically and mentally let it go.

If you're feeling anxious, come back to constant flow.
Put your hands on your heart and say, "I release the grip."

6
The More You Look, The Less You'll Find

Solitude, Stillness, Silence.

In a world full of "you must grind all the time to succeed," when was the last time you took a step back? If we are constantly running towards something, or away from it, we get stuck running in circles. These circles tend to be cycles of entrapment that make us feel like we are getting somewhere ... but really we are getting nowhere. Technically we *are* moving, however, the movement is not in the name of true progression. Do you even know why you're running? These cycles of entrapment are slick. They tend to develop silently, and are usually a result of neglecting the fundamental need of Solitude, Stillness, and Silence.

One must not be afraid to slow down. By taking a moment to sit in silence and stillness, you are giving yourself a chance to experience your life from your own perception. Your OWN INNER WORLD. When we awaken to our own perception, we begin to discover conscious and subconscious patterns that have been repeating in our lives that we no longer wish to be a part of. It is nearly impossible to navigate your own personal truth without being able to sit alone with oneself.

Discoveries far beyond the imagination are found once you make the decision to sit alone with yourself. This is because God cannot talk to you when you are surrounded by noise. When you are caught in the energetic frequencies of your surroundings, it gets difficult to determine what is the voice of the Divine, what is the voice of the mind, and what is the voice of another. Only within Solitude, Stillness, and Silence can one begin to form a connection with the true voice of the soul. No social media, no texts, no calls, no TV, no music, nothing but YOU. Once this becomes a consistent practice in your life, the voice of the Divine becomes clear.

Let's dive into a surface-level example. Have you ever found yourself running towards a relationship? Always looking for a partner to "complete" your vision. Or running away from them? Closing your heart at the notion of someone getting close to you. If you are always running, whether you realize it or not, chances are you are missing what's right in front of you.

Repeating cycles that drain us can make us feel lost and confused. Because when you find yourself in a pattern that keeps you feeling entrapped, the energy output never equals the energy input. We are giving it our best, yet still can't figure it out. When you are constantly searching, gathering, defending, moving, and creating with no results ... you end up exhausted. This is your sign to zoom out. Take a deep breath. Take a few. Allow the bigger picture to be revealed. Remind yourself : the more you look, the less you'll find. The external world does not have what you're searching for. For first it must be found within.

Break free from trying to "figure it out."
There is no finish line.
Embrace it all.
Be and let be.

If you're feeling exhausted, stop.
Hug yourself and say, "I deserve stillness, silence, and solitude."

7
Are You On Auto-Pilot?

Days turn to weeks, weeks to months, and months to years.

You look at the time passed and wonder why nothing has changed? How can all this time go by yet your dreams still feel out of reach? This may be because you hit the auto-pilot button. As humans we pick up certain physical behaviors and emotional responses to the environment around us. We are easily programmed, and this programming happens so effortlessly that we don't even realize we are running on repeated circuits. I call this auto-pilot. The most dangerous of all the auto-pilot programs are the ones built while experiencing survival mode. Survival mode occurs when your life is put at risk. Your safety has been stolen; meaning your food, shelter, and livelihood can be taken from you at any moment. When a human being experiences this type of danger, the body gets accustomed to living in fear. When living in fear, we are unable to express ourselves or fulfill our needs. We get stuck in behaviors and thoughts that engulf us in a painful lifestyle. No matter how much we may convince ourselves we are okay, deep down we know that it's not true.

How can you progress while actively choosing to stay the same? Right before this, we discussed running in circles that leave us entrapped, disconnected, and exhausted. Now, let's talk about operating from a program that hasn't been updated. This creates not only stagnation, but lag time and system errors, too. One must never neglect self-evaluation. Only through self-evaluation can we observe what is happening within our personal lives. This evaluation requires honesty, accountability, and deep forgiveness.

Personally speaking, I used to be a professional escape artist. This was my auto-pilot program, and I know many others can relate. One day you find yourself drinking, smoking, having sex, scrolling on social media ... the next day you find yourself with an addiction. You make these choices out of familiarity and proximity. Especially because these are easy choices to make in our current reality. But once those choices become a silent addiction, you sacrifice a healthy and fulfilling life. I am not here to tell you what you should and shouldn't do (that defeats the purpose of becoming unleashed). But, I am here to tell you that a vice can quickly turn into a severe situation without your conscious awareness. That thing you turn to for an escape from your reality, can become the same thing that brings you more pain than the initial challenge itself. Honor how you decide to cope with life, but be careful not to trap yourself. By chaining ourselves to addictions, we put our life in danger. Mentally, physically, and emotionally. The line between escapism and danger is thin.

Now, everyone's auto-pilot is different. Maybe your auto-pilot is something harmless. Let's say everyday you wake up to make breakfast at exactly 7am. You never miss a day. At first this gives you structure and becomes an enjoyable habit. Then, you find yourself mindlessly making breakfast everyday with no enjoyment or pleasure, just going through the motions. "Going through the motions" is the first sign of losing your sense of playfulness and excitement. This auto-pilot is not as harmful as escapism via vice, however it still creates stagnation within the mind and body. Be okay with shaking things up. Be daring. Do things differently. Update your programming.

If you're feeling stuck, come back to the truth.
Close your eyes and ponder, "Where am I on auto-pilot?"

8
Your Mind Is Your Ally

The most difficult concept of all.

We've discussed how to feel deserving, lighten up, and search for subconscious patterning. Now it's time to dig deeper. This step is the turning point in how to achieve personal freedom. If you can integrate this step, then you have gained a true understanding of how to activate your power. *TABU* is all about planting seeds to help you navigate and create a more fulfilling life. I could argue that without this step, the rest of the seeds are null and void.

The thing about the mind is that thoughts constantly come and go. The mind absorbs everything we've ever seen, heard, and felt. It's like an automatic processing machine that's on 24/7 ... while simultaneously responsible for taking action. Needless to say, when this machine gets out of control (and it will), it loses track of what's actually important in life. This is when focus becomes your holy grail. One must be willing to focus in order to form an alliance with the mind. The ability to focus on what thoughts you want to keep, and what thoughts are no longer serving you, is one of the most powerful practices you can implement.

We can never truly silence the mind. The closest we get to a silent mind is usually found within brief moments of complete relaxation and surrender. Often when you hear the term "quiet the mind", it relates to observing the thoughts, not holding on to them. Because when we hold on to thoughts, it creates more noise. Noise can be the conversations you have with yourself, the emotional reactions, the reasoning, the contemplation, the reenactments, the fantasies ... the noise is endless. For instance, let's say you sit down to meditate. You then have a passing thought about an argument you had last night. This argument makes you flustered. You don't want to think about it, but now you can't stop thinking about it ... all the things you should have said, how it made you feel, and what to do now. All of a sudden your meditation turns into a battle and you may convince yourself that it's not possible to find peace in silence. Do not give up when this happens.

What to do when we lose control? After you experience the mind waging war against you while searching for peace, you must turn to the practice of focus. Let's return to our example : the argument you had last night is replaying in your head. You can choose to hold onto that thought and ruminate in the fight ... which then creates more friction within the mind, leading to discomfort in the body, and ultimately limiting the soul's capacity for growth. Or you can pivot. You can pivot your thoughts manually by telling yourself, "I do not wish to think about that right now," or "That argument gifted me clarity about ___." You get to choose to create thoughts that cultivate peace within the mind, harmony in the body, and expansion for the soul. One of the most beautiful things about human existence is our free will. We always have the ability to make a choice.

Remember, it's a practice. When you make the choice to pivot your focus from chaos to peace, it's not easy. At first it may seem like you are being a bit delusional by shifting your thoughts. Especially in times of extreme hardship. So, I invite you to think in terms of battle. Your opponent is launching missiles at your most precious cargo. Are you going to give up and welcome the destruction? Or are you going to gently distract them to aim elsewhere? I sure hope you choose to stand up and fight. Self-preservation is key to survival. Sometimes it takes distracting your opponent (and making them your ally) in order to make it out of this game alive. At times we must swallow our pride and do things a bit differently for our own well-being.

Be gentle with yourself. It takes an extreme amount of awareness to turn your mind into an asset, not a liability; and awareness does not accumulate overnight. Once you begin to find your focus, use it to control the quality of your thoughts. Any small pivot, celebrate it. That's a big win.

I once heard this quote that said, "If your mind hasn't followed you there yet, do it for your body." Earlier I mentioned that we are forever young, but unfortunately our physical bodies are not. Our health is a blessing that cannot be taken for granted - thus we must become friends with our mind. Our mind is responsible for our quality of life, and it can unmeaningly deceive us into losing precious time. Do not fret over the past. All we have is the present. Accept it. Start right now by meeting yourself with love and kinship.

If you're feeling frustrated, come back to focus.
It is your duty to make your mind your ally.

9
Selfish is Selfless

To unleash your personal power, one must be selfish.

As we discussed, power starts within the mind. Once you tap into your personal power, you are no longer affected and controlled by external circumstances. This personal power-up can be obtained by being selfish. Not by being selfish from a place of greed ... yet selfish from a place of Love. Like the Ancient Egyptian proverb says, "The kingdom of heaven lies within You; and whosoever shall know himself shall find it." Without knowledge of self, you live in the illusion others have created for you. Your perception of self becomes distorted and disconnected.

It is crucial to be selfish. You may wonder, what does being selfish require? Being selfish requires that you reserve your time and energy for you, and you alone. Spending solo time with yourself is one of the most selfless acts one can do. Why is that? Because after you make the time to know yourself and create your own perception of life, you become a blessing to the world. Remember : it is your birthright to tap into your true essence and presence. This is one of the most humanitarian things you can do at this time. For when you bloom into your truest self, the highest calling of your being, you automatically begin to create a more peaceful and fulfilling life for yourself and all those connected to you.

Suffering is a result of separation from self. Recall a moment in time when you felt an immense amount of suffering. Chances are you were involved with people, places, and things that did not reflect who you truly are. When we get separated from our truest self, the pain is insufferable. Life becomes nearly unbearable. These instances are when we hit our "tower moments" or "breaking points". The Universe will convene to turn our life upside down (right-side up) when we are disconnected from our core essence for too long. We are not meant to live our life for others. In fact, quite the opposite. We are designed to live our life *with* others. But how can we live with one another when we don't know what we stand for? When you stand for nothing ... you'll fall for anything. Develop your backbone. Don't get lost in the sauce. And if you're currently in a state of suffering, take a look around. What feels heavy? Start there.

Learn to think for yourself. At times it's easy to mold into what others think and believe. This is a trap that will leave you forever controlled by your surroundings. It's great to listen and inspire each other, yet we must have our own base of beliefs. Our base of beliefs should be cultivated from our unique life experiences, lessons, and blessings ... not what we've seen on social media or TV. Not what we've been told to believe. We have the right to discover our own truths.

Use the power of "NO." When you want to say no, say no. Why keep subscribing to things that bring you anxiety, pain, or any type of discomfort? For the sake of peace? For the sake of being agreeable? Please know that short-term ease is not an equal sacrifice for long-term discomfort. It's better to have short-term discomfort in exchange for long-term wellness. When you embark upon this journey of selfishness in the name of selflessness, you will lose people along the way. Friends, family, and lovers may not understand where this version of you came from. That's okay. It's because this version of you has been locked away. Speak up anyways. It's time to free yourself. It's time to stand up and stand out. Be selfish. Love you for you ... and watch your whole world shift.

If you're feeling devalued or confused, come back to your center.
Look in the mirror and say, "I have the right to be selfish for the greater good of all."

10
Discipline ... NOT Dictatorship

How are you keeping yourself accountable?

It's great to know something, it's better to embody it. In order for anything to appear in your reality, one must take action ... consistently. Discipline. Discipline is required to set yourself free, the key to truly becoming unleashed. Without discipline, achievement is nearly nonexistent. Discipline, discipline, discipline. This word gets thrown at us all the time. Does that word make you cringe? It may be because you relate discipline with punishment. So, let's talk about Discipline vs Dictatorship.

Not everyone reacts well to discipline. Because who likes rules? Many prefer to rebel against them. You know those people who swear waking up at 4am makes them the most successful person on the planet? That's great for them. They found their rule to live by. But that doesn't mean it needs to be your rule, too. Most of us first learn discipline from our parents / guardians. As a child we don't get a say in what time we wake up, what we eat, how we dress, etc. Although we may disagree or find discomfort in having rules set for us, it is a valuable part of our development. If you are a young adult reading this and still have disciplinary outlines, be grateful. It's a blessing to have people that care about you and want to see the best for you. Because once you're fully on your own ... all structure disappears. It sounds fun at first, but that's when your real test starts.

What's the point? The point is finding order in chaos. Our lives are naturally chaotic ... we live on Earth; a planet of constant change and evolution. We will never be able to control everything, that would be boring. Often, chaos is where we find the most growth. However, order is responsible for our sanity and overall progression. Let's return back to our example: waking up at 4am. This disciplinary measure doesn't work for you. Does that mean you'll never be successful? Of course not. Do not create a rule that completely defies your natural state of being. You will set yourself up for failure and disappointment. The trick? Create your own rule. You are a unique individual that designs your own reality. Maybe waking up at 8am is a sweet spot for you, make that your rule, and stick to it.

Your word is your bond. Discipline goes far beyond waking up at a certain time. What's important here is that when you decide to create an outline/rule for your life, follow it. Follow it with the knowledge that it can always be changed. This is where the distinction from punishment is crucial. NEVER punish yourself for breaking a rule. NEVER make yourself suffer by following a rule that no longer applies to you. We are not perfect creatures. This idea of perfectionism is beyond outdated. Please, make mistakes. Mistakes are golden teachers, not something to be shamed for. Yes, your word is your bond. Which is why one must uphold your word even in times of failure. If you use your word against yourself, you have bonded yourself to a negative frequency that will most likely make any type of order difficult for you in the future.

Be gentle. Take the time to discover what works best for you. Find personal discipline that suits you. Also, it's best to introduce discipline with 1-3 rules at a time. If you create a long list of "to-do" and "to-follow" ... it might overwhelm you. You may find yourself rebelling against the whole list or trying to master it all at once. Resulting in either regression to no discipline or turning you into your own personal dictator. Avoid using your creation abilities to make life a prison. Set yourself free. Find balance.

There is an inner child within you that wants nothing more than to be set free. Listen to them. Follow your heart, follow your passion. Take steps towards your goals with consistent actions. Govern yourself. YOU make the rules. Just don't become a dictator. Stay clear from placing unnecessary limitations upon oneself that are unjust or unfair. Be flexible and embody unconditional love along the way.

If you're feeling oppressed or unorganized, come back to order.
Remember, "Discipline is not punishment."

11
Transparency > Secrecy

Be honest.

Have you ever lied? Have you ever found yourself in a moment where the truth was needed but you chose to be silent instead? This often happens because of fear, shame, guilt, and judgment. The previous ten concepts require honesty within oneself ... the question is, can you be honest with others, too? That's the secret to inheriting true freedom.

Imagine yourself as a mirror. Simply a reflection. Is your reflection clear and true? Or is it muddy and modified? Do you reflect what you see - or do you change your reflection to meet others' projections? If you are used to bending the truth and only sharing what's necessary, at first it may be frightening to share your truest reflection with others. It will require trust that being transparent holds the key to freedom in ways that are beyond speakable.

Free yourself from the "thought dumpster." When one lies, withholds the truth, hides, etc ... the truth doesn't just disappear. It gets stored away in a part of the brain I refer to as the thought dumpster. A literal junkyard of wastage that holds all your secrets. Let's introduce another surface-level example : your best friend asked you what you did last night. Your immediate response was, "I watched Netflix." When you know damn well you were with an ex lover ... the one that's been exiled from your life ages ago. You wanted to avoid the judgment, so it was easier to lie. Seems harmless, right? Sure. Besides the fact you just added garbage to your thought dumpster. In that moment, you had the opportunity to tell the truth and set it free. Instead, now you must remember your lie, carry the burden of withholding the truth from your best friend, and hold the weight of your emotions from the experience by yourself ... sounds exhausting. Because it is. And stinky.

Learn to speak your truth without worrying what others think of you. You are a sovereign being. You can make your own choices and learn your own lessons. The more you speak your truth, the smaller your thought dumpster gets. Otherwise this dumpster can become full of things you've withheld, and BOOM ... overflow. A messy explosion of past transgressions leaving you with nowhere to run. This happens when you have too much going on inside of you that no one knows about and you suddenly feel all alone; self-created isolation. This may cause stress and worry because you've been carrying the weight of a burden that was meant to be released. Or the opposite happens : all of your hidden truths get revealed at once and you risk losing your closest relationships. Let's avoid this. The more we practice speaking exactly what's on our mind; what's alive for us in each moment - the more we release. No one needs a full junkyard. Life is challenging enough. Let it go. No more hiding and bottling things up. Free yourself. Be transparent. Be real. Trust and be true.

*Note : When telling the truth, discernment is important. Not everyone you encounter will have pure intentions in your life. Your authenticity is a gift, it's an exclusive experience. Free yourself from opening the door for energy vampires. An energy vampire is a being that will drain your energy by any means possible ... through gossip, lies, jealousy, envy, hatred. They often arrive with a smile. Protect yourself. Lessons will be learned through these types of people and experiences, they cannot always be avoided. However, discernment will save you from unnecessary negative, low vibrations. Stay alert. Stay observant.

If you're feeling isolated or burdened, come back to openness.
I invite you to release the tension from your shoulders and relax your jaw.
Now declare, "I am safe to be transparent and honest."

12
Intention is Everything

One of the most important questions to ask yourself is, "Why?"

In this moment, why are you consuming these words written in *TABU*? What is the purpose? What is your intention? Take a moment to think about what led you here. Gain clarity behind your actions; this is a massive key in unlocking the build of your psyche.

Freedom of the mind can only be achieved with honest reflection and evaluation of oneself. One can take all the action they see in self-help books, articles, videos, and courses ... yet action is meaningless without intention. Intention is the secret ingredient that changes the whole flavor of a dish. It provides the boost we need in order to venture into new territory. Most of the actions we take are like clockwork (hence step number seven : are you on auto-pilot?). We discussed the mundane, or sometimes harmful, nature that comes with this out-dated programming. So now I ask you to take it deeper ... What is your 'why' behind it all?

Adopting a new behavior pattern will not give you the life-changing results you desire without a backing of truthful reasoning. It's a practice that takes brain power, deep presence, and curiosity without judgment or attachment to what you find. By now you must know I love providing simply exaggerated examples. So let's jump into another one : you're buying an ice cream cone. Why are you buying this ice cream cone? Because it sounds good? Because your friend invited you? Because you want to? These are all behavior-based responses. Now let's add substance and reasoning to them. You bought the ice cream cone because it sounded good and you needed to fulfill your sweet craving. Or, you bought the ice cream because you wanted to see your friend. Or, you bought the ice cream because you had a hard day and needed a sense of relief. Do you see how adding a bit more thought behind your action adds a whole new level of awareness?

Awareness has the power to set you free. Awareness is the foundation to *The Art of Being Unleashed* - and when it comes to building the grand architecture of your life, every detail matters. For when one builds without a thoroughly examined blueprint, the risk of a faulty foundation dramatically rises. Do you want to build something fast for show? Or are you willing to build something lasting with patience? Patience coincides with awareness because they both require the ability to perceive something beyond what's being shown in front of you. By taking the time to practice thinking outside your usual scope of thought, you will develop in ways unimaginable. The mind is your strongest tool in this life. Learn to sharpen it. Because once your tools are sharpened and the foundation is set with intention, the potential to build is limitless.

Let's circle back to the start. "Why?" What is the purpose of any of this? Sometimes if you dive too deep into awareness, you can be led into an era of existential wonder. You may begin to ask deeper questions that make you question existence in itself. This is when I invite you to venture back to step number three : really ... it's not that serious. Remember that the purpose of self-awareness is to discover your true intentions. It does not have to be anything more or less.

Most of you have found yourself amongst these words because you are here in the pursuit of freeing and opening up your mind. Everything you explore within these pages must be taken in appropriate doses. They are all planted seeds for your subconscious that will grow over time. Trust the process. Finding your intention should be something that is fun and empowering. Take the time to discover where you are and where you've come from. Once you've arrived, now it's time to decide - decide the place you want to create from.

If you're feeling empty or shaky, come back to intention.
FIND YOUR WHY.

13
Love Conquers All

Need I say more?

Love ... Love is Art. Love is War. Love is the strongest emotion in the world. Have you ever been overtaken by Love? The world looks brighter, your smile gets bigger, and your heart feels full. Have you ever lost Love? The world turns dark, your smile disappears, and your heart feels empty. One can say love holds immense power and pain... but does it? The absence of Love is what causes pain; not the presence of it. Love gets a bad rep because most people don't understand what Love truly is. Many were taught to associate love with coercion and control (amongst other fear-based actions). It's time to understand that Love is not necessarily action-based. Love comes from the Soul.

Love conquers all. The power of Love cannot be denied. As Martin Luther King Jr said, "Hate cannot drive out hate; only Love can do that." It's easy to be driven by our emotions. When someone causes you pain, it's natural to wish pain upon them in return. Yet that natural urge within us actually breeds more harm to ourselves and everything around us. Hate is the embodiment of a coward. Because in order to Love, one must be brave. One must rise above the primal instincts of "eye for an eye." One must make the decision to connect to the Higher Self within. One must have faith that the Universe has its own system of checks and balances. It is not your duty to play God, nor bring justice to a situation. It IS your duty to shine Love in the presence of all hate and rise above the bullshit. No matter how counter-intuitive it may feel at times.

We must actively align ourselves with Love. Love is our natural essence. Yet we exist in a world programmed by fear. Many beings lose their natural vibration of Love at a young age. Some fight to get it back, and others believe it's gone forever. But how can the same thing that birthed you be out of your grasp? It's impossible. Love is our supernova. The true wisdom of Love is only gained after we lose It. Therefore, the more we choose to consciously align ourselves with Love, the more we free ourselves from all that is fear-based. Fear-based programming is the root of all control and entrapment.

Love is the frequency of which the Universe was created. Pure creation. Everything in this world was initially created from Love. Unconditional Love. Love is Source. Love is God. Love is Oneness. Love is Acceptance. Love is Forgiveness. Love is Detachment. Love is Joy. Love is Truth. Love is Peace. Love is not an action. Love cannot be spoken. Love can only be felt. Love is the silent wind behind all miracles and blessings. Love is the ultimate protection.

It may seem complex, but really it's all so simple. We tend to make things much harder than they have to be. Ironically, this concept was the hardest to verbalize and portray. Love is such a Divine experience, and words will never be enough. I can only hope these pages captured a drop of the essence of all that Love truly is.

Think, ponder, explore. Let it flow. Let it go.
Just never forget, "Love Conquers All."

AFFIRM

Say it like you mean it.

I am whole.

I am everything I need and more.

I honor silence and stillness.

I am fearless.

I am passionate.

I am connected to everything.

I accept my circumstances.

I am joyous.

I am friends with my mind.

I only keep the thoughts that feel good.

I am enough.

I am capable of change.

I am in love with life.

I am in love with all that surrounds me.

I am worthy.

I am beautiful.

I am eternal.

I am allowed to rest.

I am aligned.

I am shameless.

I am attached to nothing.

I am free.

I release expectations.

I allow myself to play and laugh.

I honor my thoughts.

I am focused.

I am aware of habits that no longer serve me.

I am safe.

I am in love with myself.

I forgive everyone and everything.

I am confident.

I belong.

I am honest.

I trust others.

I know who I am.

I am allowed to create a life that feels good to me.

I am intentional.

I am safe to express emotion.

I am creative.

I am Love.

I am caring.

I am giving.

I am affectionate.

I am accountable.

I am strong.

I am unbreakable.

I am courageous.

I allow myself to explore.

I am present.

I trust myself.

I value myself.

I am kind to myself.

I am disciplined.

I am limitless.

I am protected.

I am unique.

I am kind.

I am forgiving.

I am generous.

I am receptive.

I am trustworthy.

I am infinite.

I am brave.

I observe, never absorb.

I allow myself to start over whenever I need to.

I embody presence.

**You can replace "I am" with
"I feel, I know, I embody, I speak, I see ..."**

Remember to create your own, too!

ACT

It's time to take action! After gaining new wisdom and insight, one must embody it through supportive action.

Don't know where to start?

Up your water intake.
Consume whole, fresh foods.
Sit in intentional stillness : Meditation.
Build Strength + Stamina .. physically, mentally, and emotionally.
Connect to your Breath. It's Life.
Stretch. Your body will thank you for being flexible.
Start a passion project.
Play more, Laugh more.
Paint. Share. Plant. Prayer.
Write about your emotions, habits, thoughts ...
Look for outdated patterning & make the choice to evolve.
Embody Grace.
Radiate Peace.

Looking for more?

Sleep in white clothing/sheets
Sleep naked
Intentionally absorb sunshine/moonlight (i.e. with presence speak, "thank you Universe/God/Creator/Angels/Ancestors/Source for this sunshine/moonlight")
Stay away from highly processed foods
Cleanliness (home + body)
Deep breathing

Study + Practice Yoga

Talk to yourself in the mirror

Stare into an animals eyes

Write with a pen and paper

Take a walk through nature without technology

Intentionally be in awe of nature (i.e. "this flower is beautiful" "wow look at that bird" - authentically speak about what catches your eye)

Bare feet on Earth

Gratitude

Offerings

Move your body freely (dance/somatic release movements)

Sing

Eat favorite food(s)

Laugh

Express all emotions naturally

Practice non-judgement of self and everything around

Massage yourself

Listen to Lo-fi beats/Hz frequencies/Jazz/White noise

Infuse food and drink with positive affirmations

What else can you think of? Get excited to explore!

EMBODY

Elemental Foundation
An exercise to aid in gradual progression and integration.

Connect with each element in one way, every day.
This tool will lead you to embodiment of your full essence.

Fire :
Wealth / Passion

What makes your eyes light up and your heart sing? Do more of that. That thing you put off because 'it doesn't seem important' or 'you don't have the time' is the exact thing you need to fuel yourself with.

Fire gazing. Look into the flame of a candle or fire - allow it to burn all that no longer serves you. Let it pave your way forward with courage and strength

Move your body. Physical movement awakens the flame within.
Walk, Run, Stretch, Play, Explore.

Water :
Health / Intention

Be intentional with your water usage. Speak life into the water you drink, bathe, and cook with. It listens and adapts. Let it cleanse and purify your body.

Consume as much water as you can every day.

Sit with a natural flow of water and watch your life be born anew.
Natural sources of water : beaches, lakes, rivers, waterfalls.

Earth :
Home / Belonging

Take a break from the modern world. Honor your place on Earth as a Human Being. The modern world is convenient and important, yes. However, it's a temporary expression. The modern world is not our true resonance.

Earth is our natural Home. When was the last time you admired a flower? A cloud in the sky? The butterfly that flew past you? The vibrance of the trees? Slow down. Look at the beauty around you. It's everywhere.

Go for a hike. Walk amongst Nature with full presence. No electronics. This is the strongest way you can honor both your physical vessel and true home.

Air :
Mind / Peace

Relax the mind. Connect to the breath.
Take deep, slow, intentional breaths whenever you can.

Go outside on a windy day. Open the windows in your home. Roll down the windows in your car. Let the air free your thoughts. Feel the air flowing through your body. Relax. Let loose and know that all is well.

Spirit :
Soul.

No rules. No guideline. Connect with this element in a way that is uniquely you. Only you know how to connect with Spirit. Only you decide your way of honoring and speaking with the unknown. The ethers are available for everyone. No one is excluded.

MAKE IT REAL

I am _____

I feel _____

I know _____

I embody _____

I speak _____

I see _____

Daily Fire Action : _____

Daily Water Action : _____

Daily Earth Action : _____

Daily Air Action : _____

Daily Spirit Action : _____

Need help filling in the blanks?
Re-visit AFFIRM, ACT, EMBODY.

Need more space?
Start a journal!

ACTIVATE

Enter the exploration part of *TABU*. Open your imagination.
Each activation was channeled with pen and paper in one-sitting.
They've been documented as-is : raw and original.

SHH

Please listen my dear ... you don't have to fear.
Love is the only weapon you need -
The ultimate frequency to set you free.
Surrender with grace and keep your pace.
We all know Life is not a race.
We need you here during this time, let your authenticity shine.
The fake is being revealed, put down your shield.
Open your eyes and open your heart
This was all a part of the deal.
You are protected - now - witness the world restart.

SPEAK

To the girl who dreams of the world,
Can't you see it's in your hands?
Just take a look.
It's clear as day.
The World is Yours.
Go Play.

RISING

Each day I wake and pray.
I vow to stay present and slay.
Thank you Source for my breath.
It's a miracle to be here - I'll never forget.
I pray for peace and happiness to rain down
Not just on me, but for all those around.
I'm grateful to be alive ...
Here's to another day opening my eyes
Father Sun shine bright.
I'm here to fight with all my might.
I surrender and release all that no longer serves me -
I am on my Divine Path ... this I know and believe.

RESTING

As I lay my head to sleep ...
I keep you next to me.
Source. Angels. Ancestors ...
I love you. I trust you. I thank you.
Release me from today as I pray.
Let my dreams take me away.
What a beautiful life ...
Within my heart there is no strife.
I ask Mother Gaia to bring me to her core
As I go to sleep to awake once more.

HUMBLE

Humbly, I run circles around your favorite.
I embody the Original Creatress.
Take a look and you'll see
Look deeper and you'll believe
Here to change the game
You'll remember my name.

Rapport with them all.
Demons respect me,
Angels protect me.
Alchemist in the Underworld,
Goddess in the Heavens,
Magician in the Flesh.
My rapport is eternal.
Here for the Most High to pave a new way,
It's time for Earth to welcome a New Day.

PASS

Just because I'm strong enough to
Fight my demons and yours too,
Doesn't mean I have to.

I was taught that love is self-sacrifice
When that's not right ...
Went my whole life without that insight.
Now I get to put that weight down,
And instead -
Lift up my crown.

NAIVE

They talk, they laugh, they stare
Yet in the face of my pain, none could bear.
I was left in a pool of my own blood
And still had to get myself up to run.
Along the way, I was searching for aid
I'd scream,
"I'm bleeding. Help me, please. Can't you see?"
Yet none believed the Mystery of Me.
Others called me foolish and naive.
When truthfully I was just coping with what was underneath.
For when you don't look like what you've been through,
Others assume you just can't follow through.

TURN OF EVENTS

Wheel of Fortune
Fortune of the Wheel -
Here to spin me into a new world
The world of Destiny,
Miracles galore
To infinity I soar

Wheel of Fortune
Fortune of the Wheel -
Grant me with your grace
While I transition into a new me
Same heart, same soul, same mission
I send the Divine kisses

Wheel of Fortune
Fortune of the Wheel -
My time is here
So I know no fear
Time to show the world whom + whose I am
Trailblazing the path ahead
In my power I stand.

As above, So below
And still I rise, Behold.
Wheel of Fortune
Fortune of the Wheel -
I give thanks
For now + ahead.

HOPE

Love come to me,
Love set me free.

Love speak to me,
Love let me see.

Love touch me,
Love make me believe.

I trust and I surrender
To whom I write this love letter.

For this new beginning, I am ready.
Ready to open my arms,
Ready to open my heart.

Love come to me,
Love set me free.

PRAYER

May all truths be revealed to me that have been kept at bay.
Reveal to me my enemies
And strengthen my gifts.
The road shall be opened at my command now,
Healing all soul parts to speak my truth with no doubt.
Remove me of fear -
The past may not come near.
For I have set myself free -
The Tigress Unleashed.
Lead me to my Divine Destiny,
For I am ready to speak.
With love as my only weapon,
I transmute us all to Heaven.
Asè. Thank you. I love you.

ROCK BOTTOM

I'm afraid the Devil has sunk his teeth in me
And I can't escape
My soul has already been sold
The price was bold
Yet still they paid
Oh how they love their little game.

BANISH

I banish all that no longer serves my highest good.
I call all my power to me now.
I declare I am free.
Bondage, Never.
Limitless opportunities, Forever.

GODDESS

I once met a lord who split the two seas.
In the middle he found me.
Tranquil and still, not a worry in the world.
He asked, "who put you here?"
I said, "myself, why do you fear?"

How could such a beautiful treasure be in hiding?
Hiding!? How did you not know where to find me?

I stay in between two worlds
My heart in a constant whirl.
One with the Universe, I stay creating pearls.
Why come find me on accident?
Your heart must've been yearning for peace -
That's the only way you find me.
So tell me ... are you here to set me free?
Why marvel at an ancient goddess?
I have what you need - you must ask me.

Meeting me between the two seas was the ignition
So tell me, what's your position?
Release me back to my flow.
For now I must go ...
One day you'll understand why you left the land.

ABORT

Baby, oh baby.
One day I'll meet you.
You've tried a many to come too soon.
Nonetheless, please know I love you.
Baby, oh baby.
I feel you.
Your favorite color is blue.
Like the tide under a full moon.
Baby, oh baby.
I know the day I can nourish you will come.
Thy Kingdom come, Thy will be done.
On Earth as it is in Heaven.
You are my Heaven on Earth. Trust me.
Baby, oh baby.
Will you forgive me?
I mourn your short-lived existence.
Now and past-tense.
Baby, oh baby.
You are a legend in the making.
We've done this before.
In the physical we will meet again.
For now I have to go ...

FCK THIS

Am I too broken?
Is it too late?
I don't mean to be funny,
But I think something is wrong with my brain.
When the beauty fades
It's nothing but pain.

I'm like an ancient vase that's been smashed
Left to make my glue from scratch
A timeless delicacy
Left looking like a piece of trash
A beautiful disaster
Worth more than cash

The glue is now made;
Yet I hesitate.
Wait.
Am I too broken?
Is it too late?

RABBIT HOLE

What truths have I been denying?
On my own life I've been spying.
Guidance, direction, structure, please.
I am on my knees.
Ashes to ashes here I am again.
Ah... transformation, my old friend.
It's nice to see you again.

As I enter this chapter, I can tell it's different
This time around ... I'm getting the job done.
Proud. Hopeful. Forgiving.
Yes ... you can stop spinning.
It's okay. I know it's unclear, but
Nothing to fear because Source is my steer.
Breathe. Let it go.
It's okay. This I know.

There's levels to setting yourself free.
You are almost there ... Release me.
Limitless reality.
I'm asking for clarity.
Stillness? Action? Sleep? Endurance?
Risk? Schedule? Boundaries? Run?
So many emotions and feelings
I've never felt like this before.
I throw my hands up and surrender
To this ebb and flow.
Divine Timing. The clock is winding.
Follow me down the rabbit hole ...
How deep can we go?

HOLY

Divine Justice, it's time to reign down
Making amends and placing my crown
Who knew it would come to this?
I'm a quarter of a century in ...
Somethings got to give
Holy Fire, Holy Water
Divine Mother, Divine Father
Let thy presence be known
For I know I have not been alone
Let me see, let me feel, let me speak
I wish to reach a new peak
A peak of alignment and power
Letting all fear be devoured.
I'm patiently waiting here
I know my time is near -
In fact, it's here.
The time is now,
To your Divine essence, I bow.

CAUTION

Slow down, my child.
You're moving too fast.
Embrace the pace of grace.
I see you are steadfast.
Loyal to your mission.
Running towards ascension.
Yet don't you know?
You're already where you want to be.
Open your eyes to see.
The Divinity is always within thee.

ALCHEMY

Leave it to me,
The keeper of the key
To set many free
To be waiting for the next day
I press play now
This moment deserves a bow
For I am evolving rapidly
Do not be deceived
By what no longer is
The purification is handling biz
So just breathe and
Welcome the arrival of me

SIMPLICITY

The wind kisses my face
Wrapped in the sun's embrace
Listening to the songs of the birds
Not a worry in the world
Running water down the stream
This life is like a dream

CHILD OF GOD

Remove all blockages swiftly
Remove it all with grace and ease
I am ready for my tribe to find me.
I approach you humbly,
I have much to learn,
Yet much to offer.
I release myself from all people, places, and things
That tried to devour me.
I am blessed by God's will.
No matter what - I see it through.
But here comes the good part -
Golden and White.
"Enough" they scream.
"Don't touch my child of Destiny"
It's time to be free.
Freedom let it ring,
The real kind.
Unleash the beast ...
That would be me.
Remove the veil and
Release the truth.
Let your light codes run loose.
Looks like it's my turn ...
Duck, Duck, Goose.

SOLO

The ones that come back for me,
Those are the most interesting.
Never ready to see it through,
Until they couldn't find me in you.
The lover in me understands,
The warrior would rather throw hands.
Truthfully, I'm indifferent.
Since birth I've been on a solo mission.
Who wants to help me for me?
Who wants to help me for them?
The truth always gets revealed.
I just sit back and listen -
Find me watching the stars glisten.
I forgive them for not seeing me,
The pain and confusion actually set me free
I forgive them for being late,
I know what it's like to fall for bait.
Heaven on Earth is my Divine Destiny.
For you and me.
Oneness is all I see.
Only time will tell,
Because the real always prevail.

FRAUD

"I love you" stops meaning much
When you don't keep in touch
Constantly pulling on my energy
Without saying a word to me
The ultimate mystery
Do you actually care about me?
That's hard to believe
The only options left are
Come and see me
Or set me free
You broke my heart
And confused my mind
It's time to release me from this bind
If you truly love me,
This is the worst way to show it
How long do you expect me to wait?
I hate this game.
It feels delusional to put my trust in you
You've never seen it through.
Hot and cold. Hot and cold.
It's sickened me to the bone.

FANTASY

I love love,
Especially the love that runs.
It leaves me to my imagination
Of what could be, the endless possibilities.
I stay in a fantasy,
Because deep down I don't believe it could happen to me.

One day I will find a love that doesn't run,
A love that shows me its here to stay.
For now, I stay safe in my own embrace
I'm on the Divine's pace
But until the end of time
I will always love love.

LISTEN

One thing about me?
I understand my assignment.
I've been about it since birth.
No one can take away my essence
Because it's pure, it's true
My soul cannot be duplicated
One of one - that's for sure.

I used to talk too much,
Now it's hard to keep in touch.
If you only could see the depth of this mission -
I set myself free with my own permission
I don't want what they want,
All you have to do is listen.
I'm meant to trailblaze
And clear the world from this haze
Chosen to touch the souls of many,
I was born ready.
Find me gliding through the galaxies,
I'm right where I'm supposed to be.
Divine timing is at play,
Soon you will see there was never a delay.

VESSEL

The ones who can see me are the most dangerous
They know who I am and arrive as best dressed
I am a vessel of God.
My light never runs out
It shines bright even when it's dark out
A light in the dark attracts the moths
How many must burn before they learn?
They come to me with their soul's yearn
Sometimes I get lost in the effect I have on others
And forget the light comes from me
There is no other to set me free
Release the shackles of this perception
Love is my only weapon
Actually ... no more weapons.
No more war.
That's me staying true to my core
I love it all. I feel the thrill of life around me
Another day closer to my Destiny
Nothing can stop me ... not even me
With flames I bathe
And watch the ashes float away
Being misunderstood could never stop me from being brave.

REIGN

No one gave me my flowers,
So I gave them to myself.
They couldn't believe I made a garden,
They thought I would harden.
Instead I became softer,
Softer in Heart -
Stronger in Soul.
Sitting in my blossom,
Moving on without them.

Rain, rain, please won't you stay?
Purify my mind, nourish my soul.
You do it like no other,
I love when you come around.
I know you rain down blessings,
Blessings of my Righteous Reign.
Rain, rain, please won't you stay?
Wash the Earth, clear the path.
I surrender to your storm,
A silent brew, leading to a seductive rule.
You know me - ready for it all.
Let's ball.

BEASTY

My beast, my shadow, my love
Why must you hold on?
You tell me you own me
Yet you don't know me

I control how far this goes
I always have
You brought me the deepest of pains
Just to reveal I have the reigns

Being there for you at the cost of my sanity
It just doesn't sit right with me
I tried to tell you I'm One of One
No one can do what I do
But if you refuse to meet me halfway
I can't help you

My beast, my shadow, my love
Why must you hold on?
Our union would bring destruction to the world
This I know to be true.

DISTRACTION

Coming back again for me it seems
What do you want for me?
You sound different
But deep down I know you're the same
I fell in love with a beast that couldn't be tamed
Yet my heart still drops when you call my name

Let all illusions fall
My Higher Self is standing tall
No fear, my past is in the rear
All I need is for things to be clear

Do not distract me from my purpose
I see green through the surface
What does this all mean?
I guess I'll give you a chance to tell me

I am the strongest, down to the bone
My Destiny is set in stone

FLOOD

If only you could see
How deep this really is for me
My whole life starting anew
Feeling like it's out of the blue
Unleashing my truest expression
Using love as my only weapon
I didn't realize how long I was in my shadow
In the darkest of nights looking for a rainbow

How long did they take my sight from me?
Its feels like centuries
But now they can't get in my way
My blessings are flooding in with no delay

Like rays of the sun shining through fog
All negativity be gone
The ocean waves bring me peace
Letting me know to release my reach
Loosen the grip
Because the wheel is getting whipped
Karma is in my favor
She's not saving me for later

The rebirth is here
So I know no fear
Let that be made clear

777

Lighter and lighter. To my Divine Destiny I go.
Where I stop nobody knows
No weapon formed against me shall prosper.
I am royalty. Here with an infinite offer
One of freedom and prosperity.
For the world, not just me
That's why I'm patient
Because the best has not come yet
My life will change in a flash of an eye
Everything I said I would be
So for now I continue down the path I'm shown
Because as I walk, I'm seeing my flowers grow
Stalks coming above ground
Waiting for their fruits to be found
No stress, no worry, no hurry
I'm right where I'm supposed to be
Feel the rebirth in the air?
As everyone stares... I don't seem to care
I know who I am
Let my ancient roots bare
For it's been a long time coming
The Tigress has been set free
Tis the era of my becoming

LEGACY

A major shift in the air
Who cares if they all stare?
My wings are being unbound
A rebirth so profound
Ancient wisdom on a mission
Never breaks, never folds
They are starting to listen
The truth be told

Their weapons make me stronger
I'm a walking transmutation of reality
They think I don't see, don't know
But the Divine never withholds
It won't be much longer ...
Haven't you heard of Divine Destiny?
The time is now
I will take my bow

Life is just getting started
Thank you God for not letting my heart harden
I believe in miracles, pure and true
I've seen the Underworld, now Heaven is to be my new
Here to leave a Legacy of Love
As below, so above

PURIFY

Purify my mind body and soul
Let all that no longer serves me go

Release me from this pain
I have so much to gain
I vow to fight for what I deserve
No matter what's been shown to me in this world

Purify my mind body and soul
Let all that no longer serves me go

Release me from this cage
Let me rise with rage
Rage for what's been taken from me
Now is the time I must set myself free

Purify my mind body and soul
Let all that no longer serves me go

ILLUMINATE

I'm not perfect - but I'm not my mistakes.
Yellow roses illuminate my shadow.
In the depths of the belly of the best - I see me.
How did I get here? Living out of fear.
I observe and release. Knowing I'm beauty and the beast.
Two makes one and that's why I run.
Together the power is immaculate, heaven sent
But the world doesn't understand it yet
So I've been hesitant.

Making love with every second of life.
Embracing peace and shielding strife.
I hold my breath knowing I must carry my knife.
Because in this world everyone is out for your life.
I trust the process although it's a lot to digest.
I hope I'm doing this right,
My heartbeat is the only thing that tells me I'm alive
That and the sway of the trees ... I know they're with me.

DESTINY

I am protected from all enemies
Seen and unseen
I am who I say I am
Success is destined for me

I can't move like them
My heart is too deep

I feel their attacks and send back love
Why use magic?
When I told you I am the Magick
Everything sent to me transmutes to a higher frequency

My soul is ancient
I am not familiar with this world
The people are so cruel
Yet still I envision a righteous rule

A compassionate reign was always the plan
Once it reveals itself, again I will say -
I am who I say I am

God is about to clear my name, I feel it
Access to me no longer, I speak it

WHY

Tears fall down my face
My heart slows its pace
At least I know I'm alive
Because these days I've been asking why
I'm tired of feeling defeated
My heart wide open for no reason
Sitting here feeling beaten but
I need to get up, it's the change of season

No one is coming to save me
It's clear to see
Another hit I'll take on the chin
Keeping my heart from turning to tin
It's my turn to catch a win

One day they'll believe
But right now they can't see

Who's to blame for this wicked game?
I just want to be free with the world embracing peace
I don't want to ask why - I want to fly

STONE

Why does it feel like I can't breathe?
Don't come near me

Your spirit is familiar
Why didn't I see?

You're here to drain me of my energy,
trying to delay my Destiny

Yet my fate is sealed in stone
Why do you think I'm so comfortable walking alone?

RA

Unleashing from my own cage
It's selfish to hold in this rage
May it shine the brightest light
To heal with the greatest might
Distant no more
Bring me to the shore
Split the sky and the sea
The birth of me
Here to hold space for our sun god to return
And he shall - he never misses his turn
Spoken as it is stated, so it is done
Let the enemies know they should run
What I have done tonight cannot be undone
I am the One

SAVIOR

Don't save her
She don't wanna be saved
Don't save her ...
But wait
What if she does?
What if she could never rely on anyone else?
What if her life has more stories than a bookshelf?
What if her front is so strong no one can see the truth?

The truth being she's dying to be set loose
She dreams of being free
Yet won't ask for help finding the key
Instead she stays locked in a false reality

In fact she's made many keys
But won't try any because she doesn't believe
that she can set herself free

Lifetimes of wisdom locked behind this door
Will her life be restored?
Someone come pick her up off the floor.
Save her
She wants to be saved
Come save her ...
Before it's too late.

FIGHT

Why do you always come back for me?
I wish you could just let me be
Are you in love? Am I your drug?
If so, then why don't you treat me like the one?

As I build my legacy, they all come for me
I wish they would let me be
Is your support true? Or are you using me as a projection of you?
I let me guard down to get beat black & blue

The more light I unlock, the darkness knocks
Remember me? Please let me in ... Their voices don't stop
My heart is so big that my vision blurs
I begin to taste freedom then my voice slurs
My physical body gets stuck between worlds

I don't need permission to be set free
So why do I expect someone else to hold to key?
From now on I live in the light to observe the dark - not the other way
around
I'm winning this fight round by round, pound for pound
I make me proud, it's time to take leaps and bounds.

CATALYST

I fed egos I should've starved
The feast of my love has gone too far
I feel like I'm living in a dream
Who really loves me for me?
And I refuse to chase
Most of them just want me in my proper place
So meet me in the middle,
Only there you'll find the answer to my riddle

I'm sitting at the head of the table
Why has my heart been so unstable?
From living in hell I supposed
To each of my foe - I already know
I feel the grit of the teeth,
Then I know it must be me

I see so clearly yet can't connect
The pain I know best.
On this road I've been alone.
Wild to the bone.
I am a catalyst of change.
You'll never be the same.
Thank me or hate me.
I guess that's my game.

TRUTH

"Why feed a girl's light that already shines so bright?
She seems so naive, do you see what she believes?
I wish to dim her glow, so instead of love I'll throw blows."

But that was never my story.
Remember life before me?
I shifted your frequency yet still you doubt me.
It's too late for amends now, I've already placed my crown.
Gained all this wisdom and built my kingdom.
So thank you for all the lessons.
One day you'll see why love is my strongest weapon.

Don't let the absence of my presence cause false projections.
You only got triggered by your own reflection.

I'm human too, who do you think has been getting me through?
The Divine Truth.
I've been busy winning ancient wars
I'm telling you to this life there is much more.

Tigress Unleashed, I'm on the run.
Never been the two ... always The One.

FUELED

I feel the new energy coming in like a whirlwind
Glimpses of the past reimagined
Who would've guessed it. Lesson after lesson
Enjoying the journey by staying present
Everything else doesn't exist, past tense
So how does it feel so real?
How many places can I be at once?
It must be a lot. My gut has a hunch
Let me fly like a bird in the sky
Unbind my wings and set me free
Only I have the key
No one else is responsible, don't you see?
I can make the world stop by just being me
What is real and what is made up?
Between the void + the infinite I stay stuck
The Queen of Duality. Which side is mine to claim?
Both. Only within both will I find my reign.
No more pain. For pain turns to fuel
Fueling up for a peaceful rule
Time to reimagine it all.
Because this time I do not fall
This time I turn life into a ball -
The grandest one of them all
Let all that does not serve me fall

DONE

My essence is beyond this realm in time
The love I carry is infinite, my heart endlessly wide
Good karma is here
So I know no fear, for I know my time is near

Most weren't ready for my frequency
They couldn't see me.
What they saw was a mirror.
Reflection. One's biggest fear.
They'd look for cracks in the glass and blame it on me
Friends, family, foe...
They all know.

I was raised by the Divine, that's why my heart shines
It can't break - only grow. Ancient magick is all I know
The void and the infinite together as One.
The suffering is done.

RUN

Rebirth Me.
Set me free.
Release the old to welcome the new.
To my Destiny I stay true.
My strength and will power is unmatched.
Awaken the beast within -
Run me a fire bath.
With flames I bathe and
watch the ashes float away
New layers come to the surface
All with the same passion + purpose
But this time I'm unshaken.
My heart can't be taken.
Me first. No more hurt.
Rebirth Me.
Set me free.
Tigress Unleashed.
From my karma bonds I've been released.
Spoken as it is stated. So it is done.
Let them all know that they should run.

CHOSEN

Cracking under pressure? Can't relate.
Through the darkness I skate.
I looked the Devil in the eye and made him fall in love.
Both light and dark fit me like a glove.
This is why I was chosen,
They know I can't be broken.
I transmute more than the human mind should handle
Nonetheless, I stay in my saddle.
Gliding through the galaxies,
Earth is my favorite place to be.
The people are broken and in pain.
I know this because I feel everything.
Otherwordly, there are no words for me.
All I want is to set you free.
The chosen one, cannot fake it.
If we work together, we can make it.

RUTHLESS

Baby, I'm ruthless. I know.
When's the last time I had fun ... feel like I'm bout to blow.
Come over with wine and tree,
I need you to catch a vibe with me.
Show me how to relax and make me laugh,
Grab my hips while I throw it back.
Please don't get caught up by my past -
I was living too fast.
But I was forced to slow down -
Look at me now.
If you don't believe me, you can leave.
This is your warning, don't come back for me.
The depth of my emotions, deeper than the sea.
Intensity and passion, that's all me.
Give me your all or none at all.
Tell me, are you ready to fall?
Unconditional love and loyalty is all I crave.
Tell me, are you brave?
I don't mean to burn you with my fire.
I just want to elevate us higher.
If you deny my flame there's really no one to blame.
Just know my heart for you will turn to stone.
Baby, I'm ruthless. I know.

WILD

I am in perfect balance - release and let go.
I no longer look at myself as moving slow when
I need a second to rest and reload.
Integrating all parts of myself - I am whole.

I never hold back, I give all of me.
That's what makes me so free.
Unconditional Love and Expression.
Do you feel all this passion?
I told you Love is my only weapon.
Get into it yuh - it's the newest fashion.

Sit with me and see things differently.
I'm not judging you, so don't judge me.
We both have the power to release.
It's called *The Art of Being Unleashed*.

Come run wild by my side.
I'll lead through the day and night.
I understand this ride.
And overstand all it takes is a little might.
I got out of my own way
Now I can show others we're allowed to play

Channeled on the day *TABU* was born.

VIBRANT

I understand you want my essence in your presence -
I'm oh so precious.
But are you willing to pay the price?

I only accept fierce love and firm support
Calculation isn't an option, you'll lose your rapport.
If you can't handle me, don't fight for the spot ... crumbs are left to rot.

The vibrance is bright -
But I can tell that's what you like.
I like it, too. That's why you must show me you're true.

The vibe is limitless, infinite if you will
What's your intention with me?
Be honest and true or else you'll be left blue.

I'm not hesitant to leave.
Tigress Unleashed.
You've never heard of me?

OVER IT

I tried to leave once, but you wouldn't let me go.
Your words don't match your actions -
All I'm seeing is fractions.
I could've been the biggest blessing in your life ...
Instead I had to pull my knife.
The cord must be cut because I've had enough.
You say your intentions are pure,
So why do you leave me constantly hurt?
I may be young but I'm far from dumb.
Nothing is adding up ...
I have my whole life ahead of me ... why would I stay stuck?

All I needed was time and affection.
Instead you ran the other direction.
I hope you find what you're looking for
Because I can't take anymore.
I know my energy is intense.
If you were just a fan I guess that makes sense.
I will not live up to your perfect expectations
To fulfill your ego I gave you a standing ovation.
I know my worth - this is true.
Say what I mean, mean what I say ... do you?
You made me love myself deeper
When it comes to my heart - I am the only keeper.

3, 2, ...

Who know I'd be sitting here in front of this mirror
seeing things so clear ... yet still so unknown
I know it's okay because I always carry my arrow and bow.
This new beginning requires major will power
within every second, minute, and hour.
I refuse to back down.
I'm looking at my Destiny, why quit now?
I wouldn't want it any other way.
I understand why I had to feel all this pain.
It's not personal -
The purpose has always been bigger than me.
I am the Wounded Healer -
I clearly see.
All of this had to happen.
I'm right where I'm supposed to be.

DAZE

I haven't written in a few days ...
My minds been in a daze.
I've been standing in my Light -
But its been illuminating the dark
Pressure makes diamonds, right?
You hear that dog bark?

No one knows how much pain I'm in,
That's why I keep it all locked within.
Maybe someday someone will find the key -
The key to unravel me ...
My dreams are right here,
I have nothing to fear,
So tell me when does this pain disappear?

Affection is all I crave
And someone who can take things to the grave.
I've got it covered but sometimes the pain is too much to bare
If I share with you - will you even care?
This is much, much bigger than just me.
I've been running to my Destiny.
Infinite like the sea,
My soul is begging to be set free

FINAL CALL

Access to my heart is no longer.
The pain is too much to bear.
I'm tired of being made stronger.
It just doesn't seem fair.

I'd rather die alone than give another dog a bone.
My energy is too pure and precious.
Over the lessons. Let me heal in peace.
Making room for my blessings. Don't mind me.

I don't have time for these games.
You must be on your way.
I don't deserve to feel like this.
I'm the loss they always miss.

My intentions are pure, heart made of gold.
But all it takes is some pain to trigger my actions cold.
The scars on my back are bleeding and my heart barely beating ...
Back in my cave, I'm retreating.

Left to lick my wounds by myself.
This isn't the first time, I'll show you my bookshelf.
So yes I'm constantly ready to leave,
My peace means everything to me.
What will it take to make you see?

PRELIM

How do I know if you're true?
Too many times I've been left blue.
I want to trust,
But usually I'm the object of lust.
Loyalty is all I ask for.
And Honesty ... Nothing more.
I guess time will tell,
I hope this isn't just another spell.
My heart is open wide.
My love crashing down like the tide.
How do I know if you're true?
It's all up to you.

LOST & FOUND

Looking in your eyes I see lifetimes
I feel it when I'm by your side
Getting lost in the energy of what's destined to be
I've never come across a true reflection of me

I'm here to set the world free, that includes you
Set your passions on fire and watch you bloom
I wish to kiss your body, every inch
And heal your pain like a flip of a switch

Thank you for finding me again -
I missed you
A feeling that feels so true
Even though this is all so new

I won't leave you alone,
Unless you ask me to go
When you're ready to steer,
I'll be here
All love, no fear

RELATABLE

I wonder if anyone knows how it feels to be this alone
Well not alone, but grown
Not grown either because I'm still so young.
Inner wisdom ancient but still running races.
My whole life I've been on the run, but now I get to pause.
Catch my breath.
It's time for a new start, this I know is true.
I finally got my peace, now it's Me vs My Mind.
It's getting closer to me being free -
Life is giving me a chance to release all that no longer serves me ...
Me and My Destiny - a true love story
I've been ride or die since birth to my purpose
I know I'm here to be of service
To share my Light
And let everyone know it can be alright.
Everyone can heal. Look around,
Most of our wounded healers are our best teachers.
The depth I feel is intense.
Sometimes I feel like no one knows how it feels ...
But that is impossible because we are all reflections.
The higher the highs, the lower the lows -
This I'm learning to balance with Love as my only weapon.
My strength and will are unbreakable ...
Truly One of One - although all I want to experience
is being relatable.

GYPSY SPIRIT

Should I stay or should I go?
I don't know.
Time is flying by -
I'm trying to find something to hold.
Every time I find myself, I get lost again
Looks like it's time to get high ..
Because in my own mind I have a friend.

Lifted ... Gifted ... yes.
So please tell me why I feel such a mess.
I know it's going to be okay ... I'm okay but
Tell that to the side of my mind who's ready for doomsday.

I have so much faith
Yet I pace
Stuck in my mind, trying to figure it out
Lord, please release me of this doubt
Life is not a race
But ever since I've been born, I've been on the chase
Damn ... I wish I knew what this was about

A new version of me is being birthed -
much like what's going on with Earth.
Heaven on Earth is our birthright.
Opulence is the Destiny - don't you see?
This I know - and this is why I continue to grow.

The challenge may be that I'm running, running, running ...
When I need to learn how to go with the flow
I am protected
This I know - and this is why I continue to grow.
This is why I'd rather write than yell.

Stepping to the throne gracefully
I only have to accept me
After all, this is my reality
Step by step. Day by day.
I keep paving the way

Right now I need to know
Should I stay or should I go?
I still don't know.
I'm about to see it unfold.

ENOUGH

The darkness no longer suits me.
I follow God's will.
They keep waiting for me to give up ...
But you know I never will.
I always knew the purpose was bigger,
Because I'm used to living in the sky, go figure.
This is all much bigger.

I'm not here for another karmic contract.
In fact, I'm here to help keep Earth intact.
Mother Earth, our first true Mother, is in dire pain
Yet we keep letting her smother

The frequency of Love has won.
Time and time again it will never be undone.
Many of us are remembering who we truly are.
We are the stars.
Free will is ours.

I'm ready for the journey ahead.
Truth of Divine Joy, Freedom, and Love
This is home and it fits like a glove.
It's time to have fun exploring all while
Showing Gratitude for Creation's Glory.

UNBREAKABLE

The Devil had its time trying to sell my soul to the sky.
That time is over, I am the beholder.
I see what has been done and I raise you one.
Now it's time to have my fun.

I am unstoppable, not once have I not been in motion
My will power cannot be beat, don't you see?
A pure soul destined for success
I'm always giving it my best.

Black and yellow has been my fellow
Death and transformation I handle oh so mellow
My crown is placed with grace
I am at my own pace

Game over it's clear.
My past is in the rear.
Love and Gratitude I'm holding near.
Watch how beautiful I steer.

I'm coming for everything that's mine.
I control my vessel here and in the sky.
To my purpose I've been a true ride or die.
I am unbreakable - nice try.

AGAIN?

Nobody is perfect, but mistakes still hurt -
they feel like being stuck deep in dirt.
Dirty, messy, stuck.
Another mistake, just my luck.
I wish my mistakes didn't humiliate me.
I am only human after all.
Growing just like a tree
Seasons come where my leaves have to fall
Who is there to comfort me?
Who can't wait to see me drop the ball?
I feel so misunderstood.
Even though I'm standing where I knew I would.
In these moments of grief for who I was,
My mind gets lost in a buzz.
Here comes my Higher Self to stop the madness -
No regret. No shame. No one to blame.
I refuse to hold onto these feelings of sadness.
Life is just a game.
Shake it off.
I'm the boss.
I own everything about myself.
I am surrounded by wealth.
Inside and out - I continue to shine.
Dirt can be rinsed off - no more grime.
I am polished and new,
Look how much I grew.
My roots run deep and sturdy
I am in no hurry

ANCIENT EYES

I see beyond the veils of this realm.
Can't you tell?
I live by freedom and expression
With Love as my only weapon.

The mission is to inspire and set free ...
Just by being me.
It's never personal ...
Understand I'm living my Destiny.

Unwavering strength and sense of self.
One of One - there is nobody else.
I swapped the battlefield for the garden.
So when I walk away ... beg my pardon.

Intuition is the most selfless and pure energy.
That's why I never cared how I'm perceived -
Because I've always been true to me.

Pure soul. I've never moved in vain.
If I ever did hurt you - it was because of my own pain.
You are me and I am You.
All I want is for a better world to be true.

ASCENSION

Mama, did I climb too high?
I haven't been on the ground, only in the sky
Now I feel it and see it all...
Does it get any more tall?

I don't mean tall .. I mean deep.
Emotions so deep I could weep -
But I'm not sad,
Actually I'm glad to stand where I stand.

Limitless. Abundant sky.
I'm looking into my Higher Self's eyes...
Mama, did I climb too high?

DEEP END

We don't speak the same frequency.
The old me has left, can't you see?
Come join my frequency so you can hear me.

I speak fire - I see Divinity.
I need to see the world set free.
Love and Fear - that's all there is.
Energy and Light - that's all we are.

I am waiting for the day you can hear me.
I've been so alone - but that's okay
Wild Woman ... I am She.
I'll keep blazing my path day by day

If I told you a secret? Could you keep it?
Are you willing to breakthrough?
Remember, You are Me and I am You.

Tigress Unleashed. I'm on the run.
Please come have fun.
Embrace the Dark so you can see the Light
Heaven on Earth is our birthright

Creator ... thank you.
To you I'll forever be true.
Help them see me like I see you
Feel the emotion ocean? Deep blue.

DEMISE

Man to me is kryptonite
This is hard to even write.
I start to lose my breath
My mind in a blur, words start to slur.
I may have never been loved by a man.
They get what they want from me and leave.
They don't even realize it's not a want - it's a need.
My soul sets them free. Ecstasy.
But what does it do to me?

I'm too precious to move how I move.
Yet I get trapped again and again.
I don't realize until it's too late...
It's the Devil. I know and can't pretend.
he uses men as his channel - bait.
he knows what makes me bite,
And he knows I'll never not fight.
I am getting wiser now, you should be worried,
I know your game and I'm done playing.
Instead, I'm praying.

My heart is full of Love, Light, and Forgiveness
So righteous.
I feel my emotional depth
I swim and swim - I'll never drown.
Good luck getting to me now.
I am Woman. I am God.
My power is mine.
I declare you release me of this bind.

THE DOUBLE

Here I go again inside my mind ...
Oh, the things I find.
Sometimes scary - sometimes fun
Lately they all make me want to run .
We can't escape this human experience.
We signed up for this - this is true.
All is One. I am you.
You are me. Do you see?
Together we stand in the fire
We raise our vibrations higher and higher
All is fair in Love & War
But something is telling me there's more
Each day I face my shadow and embrace my light
I will never not fight.
For I am a warrior, an empress ... yes.
To inspire, not intimidate is my mission.
All they have to do is listen.
All I have to do is speak
That is how I reach my peak
I walk with intention
I present myself authentically
I set wildfires. The world ablaze.
I'm ready to leave the haze.
Here I go again inside of my mind ...
Oh, the things I find.
I do not run. I do not fear.
I'll keep soaring to make things clear.

TOXIC

The grass looked greener because it was fake
I guess you had to learn that the hard way

Always chasing the next shiny thing ...
Baby, where's your self esteem?

You'd rather have shit dipped in gold
Than anything that dare challenges your soul

So tell me,
How does that plastic taste?

You always call when you need a real meal.
I'm here to nourish, that's the deal.
But for you ...
I believe revenge is dish best served cold.

CHAINED

It's a constant push and pull with my inner demons that just won't let me go.
One says, "stay" - the other says, "go"
It's hard to trust when I've been misled before.
Mislead too many times to count, an overflowing drawer.

I fight back with my soul, but I'm tired.
I'm sitting here in the aftermath of a fire.
A fire that I created and extinguished.
Who knew I had that power?

I've been in the darkness for so long the light hurts my eyes,
Sometimes I hear, "it's okay, trust me, this light won't hurt your eyes"
But once glance and the angel inside me dies.

It's a constant push and pull with my inner demons that just won't let me go.
One says, "stay" - the other says, "go"

WHOLENESS

I haven't wrote a poem in a long time ...
Or been able to cry.
Let alone look myself deep within the eyes.
Where did it all go?
When did I let my creativity become my foe?
When did I become ashamed of my sensuality?
And start running from all I can be? ...
My Divine Destiny.

I am unshakable, unbreakable, yes.
For this season too shall pass.
I whether the storm with no fear
For the rain I hold dear.
The darker the nights, the brighter the shine they say.
And my time to shine has no delay.
It's been written for me from the start.
God birthed me with his mark.
The winged mother surrounds me
Together I am the picture of Unity.
Wholeness.
What the world has yet to see.
Here comes me ...
The Tigress Unleashed.

VIOLET FLAME

By the light of the violet flame,
I declare they hear my name.
The name destined to change the course of the world.
I am that girl.
A child of God, it's true.
Destined to free me and heal you.

By the light of this White candle,
Purify my manners.
Shine clarity on my purpose,
May I fulfill my potential before the world ends.
Reawaken my confidence.
Build my strength.
Show me the next steps to take.

By the light of God's love,
Peace fits like a glove.
Cover me with protection,
No more weapons.
Only truth.
I love you.

RED CANDLE

Red candle.
Red ink.
Passion, come to me.
By the light of this flame,
I announce my real name.
Spirit team, hear me roar.
For you know whom its for.
The Righteous Ones.
Amongst those who Won.
Won the Battle of Love.
And it's only just begun.

Red candle.
Red ink.
Passion, come to me.
For the good of all and harm to none.
May We All see more Love.
I call upon miracles to rain down.
Make it Clear and Loud.
Gracious and Fierce.
Soft yet Sure.

Red Candle.
Red Ink.
Passion, come to me.

HOME

I feel the Earth speak to me;
As gentle as a summer breeze,
As wild as a Lioness
Running through the trees.
As intricate as a spider's web,
And as loyal as a dog to its best friend.

I feel the Earth speak to me;
How lucky must I be?
To know the land's language,
Finding ancient gems in hidden places.
Every day is a vacation,
Yet surrounded by familiar faces.

I feel the Earth speak to me;
I hear silent frequencies.
As I dance amongst the tidal waves,
I watch Man tell me to behave.
One of None. I will not be done.
Until God tells me my time has come.

I feel the Earth speak to me;
Take some time to sit with me and you will see.

BIG MAN

I wonder what it would be like to be the girl that's chosen. When my MO is usually the girl that's broken. The fun girl. The down bitch. The one that could care less if you're in a ditch. I'll listen to your pitch. Your pitch, the plan on how you dream to leave that ditch. He says baby, watch this.

I open my eyes and look for a surprise. Digging deeper and deeper, I wonder what's on his mind. Can't he see how dirty he is making me? Yet he can't see. Money is on his mind, see? Digging for diamonds and uncovering buried bones. The bones tell a story of all those before me. Should I be worried? No, it's okay. Just stay out of his way.

Looking at this man emulate a lost dog that escaped the pound, fighting round after round, pound for pound. He's covered in dirt and scars and now I am too. All I wanted was to listen to your dreams, not get left black and blue.

I was never taught what love is. Love. I hear the word love and want to run. So instead I stay. I stay with hopes that one day the pain will go away. You sure know how to pick em, huh? Thinking you're walking the road less traveled ... well honey, you are far away from the gravel.

When will you stand up and leave? This ditch is no longer a ditch. It's a sea. A sea of despair and illusion. But wait ... does this mean he picked me? When did the ditch become the sea and why didn't I see when I had the chance to be everything I wanted to be. Instead I was focused on my broken. Claiming I was broken and looking to be chosen....

I'm tired. Sleepy. Uneasy. This has become too much. I'm sinking. Wait. He screams. His eyes light up. Amongst the bones a treasure was shown. A treasure shiny enough to wipe him clean. Would you look at that? This man has been born anew. He rises from the sea like he never saw what was underneath. Looking down at me, he says .. you expected to come with me? A laughter so loud it booms. Poof. Aloof. Alone. Back to my original MO.

BELIEVE

The woman who walks on water is the water, don't you see?

Never the wave, always the sea. See? If that went over your head, then you're not ready to understand what an Ancient Godis offers to the land.

Although her tides may change, it's wise to never misuse her name. For she is the infinite and the void all in one. There's no use in trying to run. Everywhere you turn, you'll realize she is the only one. Because her reign is never done. Done? No. In fact, we've just begun. The war has already been won. Yet not in the 3D - there's a slower processing speed.

There can be no more "I" and "Me". There's only room for "WE". So if you're not on board, I kindly ask you to leave. I'll even say please.

For if you're not here for God's plan, nowhere near me may you stand. I'm just the messenger... Don't take it out on me.

The woman who walks on water is the water, don't you see?
One look in her eyes is all it takes to Believe.

JOURNAL ENTRY
11.30.22

I surrender my mind to positive thoughts.
I am on a beautiful wave of Divine Abundance.
I am everything I need and more.
I do not concern myself with the past or future.
I am fully present.
I honor my body.
I honor my life.
I am protected and supported in ways I cannot comprehend.
I am grateful for all the amazing things and people in my life.
Infinite opportunities are ahead of me.
Creativity and play are available to me now.
I am my own inspiration.
I get inspired by the art that is life.
I know ground-breaking success is my Destiny.
I will get there no matter what path I choose.
I stay wild and free.
I let myself explore again.
I allow myself to laugh, dance, and sing more.
I fuel my body and mind with Divinity.
I love myself.
I release all that tries to weigh me down.
I am patient, calm, and grounded.

JOURNAL ENTRY
4.24.23

Just two years ago was the first time I felt safe in a long time. It was a blessing. But the blessing came with a curse. Me. I was forced to face my life head on ... by myself. Every night I was the one holding myself down. Many nights I would cry alone and beg for mercy. Many days I would completely dissociate out of my body. Time ceased to exist. Yet with that came many joyous moments of peace, dance, good food, and sunshine. Duality. Duality of the human experience.

I have grown to know the Light + the Dark quite well. On the extremities of both ends. That is why I am accepting and non-judgemental to every soul I encounter, because I know what Life can be like and feel like. My place here is to inspire and leave a Legacy of Love. Because Love Truly Conquers All. Love ... All. All is One. We are just reflections of the one true Source. That is why we are supposed to work together - not against each other. Let people be themselves - that's the only way we can truly grow. Every being must know their Soul. From there, Authentic and Enlightened co-creation begins. Nu Earth.

I tend to do that a lot, too. I go from talking about myself to the collective. I often find this happening. And that is how I know this is all much larger than me. My experiences have made me who I am. It has all happened for a reason. I accept this and I love this. I am ready to share this. But what holds me back from moving on is me. Deep down I am still angry, sad, hurt, and numb from everything. I've needed true connection in my life and I've been doing this alone.

Anyone who truly has love for me and tries to help me, I don't know how to tell them what I need, or how to trust them fully. Because I've seen too much fake love turn into envy, greed, and mental warfare. I've seen myself attracting and accepting people who treated me poorly because no one was there to show me any differently. Besides God. God never left me. In every situation and experience and relationship I've ever had - I've been shown the way. The way to Love and Unity. With no worry of how it's perceived.

I stopped living based on reality and external things. I learned how to live based on my Soul's evolution. With Angels and Ancestors and Forces beyond my comprehension supporting me and making their presence known everyday. I would be lying if I said I wasn't blessed . I am immensely blessed and don't take this for granted. This is why I always shine my light for good. My intention has always been to uplift and inspire since birth.

I know how to stand in the Light. Strong. And I learned how to stand in that Light in the Darkest of Nights. My purpose is to help others find their Light, too. What makes you, you? That is Heaven on Earth. That is why I keep focused. That is why I feel everything with such depth... Because I am here to believe in and create a better world. Life shouldn't be like this. I know I'm not the only one experiencing their own sense of suffering.

We have the power to heal and remove ourselves from suffering at any time - yet we are in a world that is designed for us to perish. This isn't life ... it's death. And only We have the power to change that.

FAREWELL, MY FRIEND

In this busy world, it's rare to hold another's attention.
Please know that if you've given TABU an ounce of your time and energy ...
I Thank You With My Whole Heart.

TABU is like a child of mind, a special love. It's been an absolute honor to share it with you. This book almost didn't see the light of day because of judgement and shame. Despite the internal and external pushback, I pushed past my fears and decided to release it. My hope is that this book provides you the fuel to push past your fears, too.

I encourage you to become deeply fascinated with the human experience - no matter how difficult at times. Feel everything. Experience it all, even when others seem to misunderstand you. Ignore the disrespect, too. It will always be a process. I pray you learn to love yourself along the way. Trust your creations. Be free.

Thank you for witnessing the birth of me.
The Legacy of Love.
My intent is pure and true.

May this piece of art inspire you. Return to it as much as you wish to.
TABU is designed to aid you in remembrance.
Never black and white. Never set in stone.

Cheers to a joyous journey of self-discovery. Happy Remembering.

Love Deeply,
Prolific. The Angel Warrior.
A simple creature with an ancient soul.

ABOUT AUTHOR

Meet Prolific.
The Angel Warrior.

Prolific, formerly known as Jessica Webber and Jessa Sparacino, was born in 1997 and has lived a life filled with profound experiences. While she chooses to keep the intricate details of her personal journey private in this work of art, she offers a glimpse into her metamorphosis :

From birth, Prolific's life moved at the speed of light, relentlessly rushing forward until the world came to a standstill in 2020. During this global pause, she confronted the reality of who Jessica Webber, or "Jess Webb," had become. This period of deep suffering led her to realize that part of her identity needed to be released for true healing and alignment with her destined path to be reached.

Embracing her great grandmother's last name, Sparacino, she became Jessa Sparacino—a chapter marked by strength, balance, and renewal. As a model, boxer, dancer, yogi, and spiritual enthusiast, Jessa Sparacino embodied a loving heart and youthful spirit, full of ancient wisdom yet worldly naïve. This transformation empowered her to reclaim her life, choosing self-love and authenticity above all else.

In October 2021, during this period of rebirth, she channeled *TABU* (*The Art of Being Unleashed*). In a single night, she envisioned the complete purpose of this work. Little did she know, this passion project would require years of dedication and personal alchemy before it could make its way into the world. Before her project could be set free, she first had to free herself.

Now, in 2024, she emerges as Prolific—a name gifted to her by God when she dedicated her life to service. With the release of her first book, she embraces her identity as the Angel Warrior, Lioness of God, and Tigress Unleashed. The Goddess of many names. Prolific is uniquely connected to the collective consciousness. Her words ease the mind and fuel the soul. Most importantly, her creations have just begun.

"Whole. Free. Happy with How it All Came to Be."

TAKE THESE WITH YOU

* Life is a Gift.
* You are Worthy of Freedom, Love, and Joy.

* It's okay to not have all the answers ...
The process of discovery is enjoyable ... If you let yourself enjoy it

* You are Deserving of Miracles.
* We are One. All is One.

* Keep your heart as light as a feather,
Even when tested in the harshest weather.
* Truth cannot escape the Divine, it's the Righteous design.

* Nothing ever stays the same ...
Gratitude for the highs, lows, and everything in between.
* Be Brave and stand in the frequency of Love ...
Even when it doesn't seem possible.

* We create Heaven on Earth. It's obtainable. It starts within.
* Aid yourself = Aid the world.

* Words are spells. Emotions are cues.
Thoughts are habits. Action is programmed reaction.
* No more FOG (Fear, Obligation, Guilt) ...
We need you to LAF (Love, Accept, Forgive)

* Head High, Heart Open.
* There is no final destination. You are an Eternal Soul.

* Love is not a weakness - Love conquers all.
* Wildness is Sacredness

I LOVE YOU.
Sponsored by Ancient Intelligence :
Universal Life Force Energy.

END

www.ingramcontent.com/pod-product-compliance
Lightning Source LLC
Chambersburg PA
CBHW072047090426
42733CB00033B/2447